This book is for

_____

MAY THIS BE A GUIDE IN YOUR JOURNEY TO BECOMING THE BEST VERSION OF YOURSLEF.

Wishing you the best.
Toi

Copyright © 2025 Toi Blackwell

Published by
Toi Blackwell
Level 444, Inc

All rights reserved. No portion of this book may be reproduced in any form without written permission from the author or publisher, except as permitted by U.S. copyright law.

Notice: This book is intended to be treated as an encouragement guide only and is not intended to treat any medical problems. This book is based on the author's experiences and imagination. If you have a medical problem, we urge you to seek a medical professional.

For permission requests contact Level444inc@gmail.com

Level 444, Inc
6450 Evans Dr
Unit 191
Rex, GA 30273

Printed in the United States of America
ISBN 979-8-9888749-5-9 (Paperback)
First Printing

BECOMING

WELCOME

This is your guide along your healing journey, to help you get into alignment to become the best version of yourself.

It is designed to share important insights that can help transform your life and lead you toward your heart's desires.

Many of us have faced difficult circumstances growing up. Often without healthy guidance needed to navigate important life lessons.

When we aren't taught certain skills, we operate in survival mode based on our environment and the things we saw, and now as we age through life, we develop habits through the years that have shaped us into who we are today.

It's never too late to make changes in your life.

It's all about how you view yourself. You can reset your old way of thinking and unlearn what you have seen and been taught; especially if those lessons have led to unhealthy habits.

You cannot hide behind past traumas. You must heal from them.

Embrace the new version of yourself that has learned from your experiences and no longer repeats old mistakes.

The version you are today has shaped your current circumstances.

If you want something new, you cannot approach it with old habits; otherwise, you will end up with the same results.

As you continue along your healing journey with me, let this book be your guide to assist you to get into alignment to become a better version of yourself despite any traumas you have experienced.

Amari

I will always advocate for you!

Be kind.
Autism occurs in 7/10 families ❤

CONTENTS

YOUR DESIRES	9
CHANGE YOUR THOUGHTS	11
WHAT IS YOUR ATTACHMENT STYLE?	21
FORGIVENESS	27
REPROGRAM YOUR RESPONSE	33
CREATE NEW HABITS	36
GIVE YOURSELF GRACE	40
GET INTO ALIGNMENT	42
THE POWER OF DETACHMENT	46
RELEASE CONTROL	48
YOUR LEGACY	52
YOUR PURPOSE	54
THANK YOU GOD	56
YOUR NEW YEAR	61
LOVE ADVICE	62
YOUR INNER CHILD	67
YOUR GREAT ENDEAVOR	69
YOUR PATH	70
IMPORTANT LIFE LESSONS	74
IMPERFECTLY PERFECT	78
NOTES	80
NOTES	81

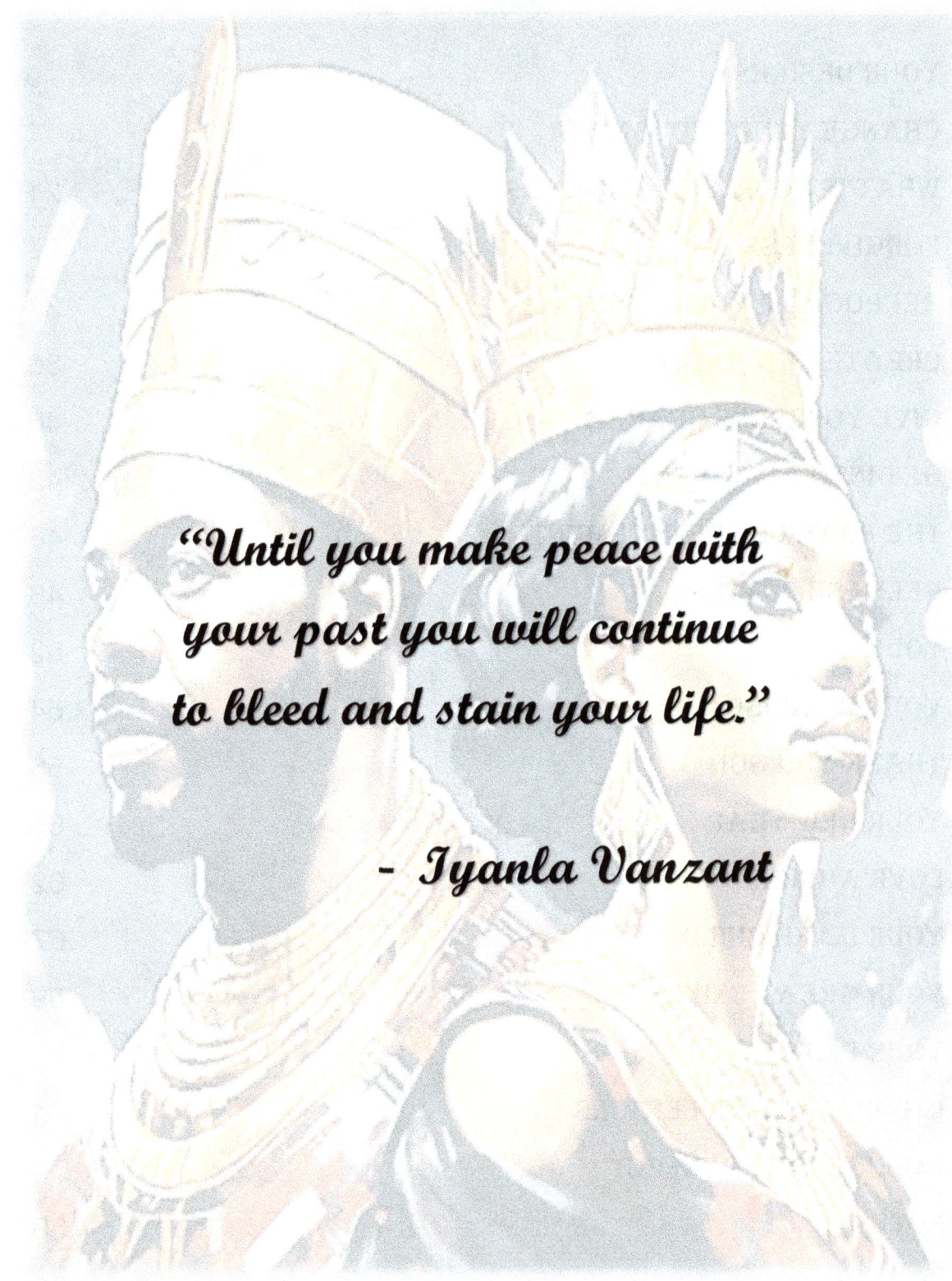

"Until you make peace with your past you will continue to bleed and stain your life."

— Iyanla Vanzant

YOUR DESIRES

You are responsible for the life you want.

The only person that can save you is yourself.

You have to know what you want, not be afraid of wanting it, and not talk yourself out of it. You have to know that you deserve to have whatever you want and do the work to set yourself up for success!

Only you can change your life.
No Excuses.
Trust yourself enough to make the best decision for yourself.

ASSIGNMENT:
Let's start your journey by asking yourself the following questions:
(write in the space below)

1. What do you desire the most today and why do you want it?

2. What do you believe hinders you from what you are desiring and what can you do to begin moving forward?

You must be honest with yourself and determine what has been working for you and what has not, because the life you currently have is based on what you have previously done.

We repeat patterns based on what was seen in our past until we make the choice that what we saw and experienced is not what we want for ourselves.

We want better!

CHANGE YOUR THOUGHTS

How you think creates how you feel.
How you feel becomes an emotion, that emotion becomes a vibration, and that vibration becomes a magnet that attracts things to you.

Everything you think comes into existence, so it is important for you to try to think of things you want to come into existence.

Everything begins in your brain. It all starts with understanding your thought process and why you have certain thoughts. For example, have you ever driven a car and realized that you accidentally went the wrong way because you are so accustomed to driving in a direction out of habit?

That is you operating in your subconscious mind.

Your brain operates in your subconscious mind 95% of the time and in your conscious mind 5% of the time. Your brain operates on what it remembers, what it has seen, what it has heard, and how things have made you feel.

Your brain does not know the difference between reality and fake reality. It only knows what is allowed to enter it, and depending on the frequency and type of information, such as, what you see in movies, TV, or social media, it will become factual and true.
This is attributed to the results you currently have in your life today.

You can reprogram your brain to believe that it can have whatever it is that you are wanting the most. You must get into the habit of protecting your mind. Your brain already has information embedded into it from a child.

Who you are at your core is from what you've seen, heard and experienced between 1 and 7 years old. Whatever you saw or experienced in that time frame is how your core beliefs are developed.

If you were sexually abused, lied to, felt unheard, were physically abused, your mother or father wasn't around causing you to have to depend only on yourself, or perhaps you experience lack, this is all information that gets embedded into your brain and develops your core beliefs.

Your self-worth and what you deserve is created at that time, and begins to shape your behavior and how you interact with people.

What you experienced at a young age, causes where your brain will subconsciously focus.
Your brain will focus so much on what it doesn't want that you will draw in what you don't want.

Whatever you focus on is what you will bring into your life.
Many people will call it manifesting. It is all intentional energy. Even praying is intentional energy.

You must reprogram what was taught to you, because what was taught to you was to the best of their knowledge and their experiences.

You start reprogramming your brain with your thoughts first.
Every thought that enters your mind. You can consciously control it.
How you feel is a product of how you think, and your thoughts can be changed at any time just by changing the picture.

If you want to begin to reprogram your brain, start with the following steps:

First, begin changing your sleep regimen. Your level of sleep determines the amount of change that you can expect. Sleep and focus go hand-in-hand.

Second, change what you allow to enter your brain. For example, at night instead of having your TV on a that plays commercials when your subconscious mind is most receptive to information, you should listen to sounds or affirmations that will feed your subconscious mind the information it needs to create the reality that you want.

A brain that needs healing can force you to create things that are not there.

ASSIGNMENT:
If you are serious about becoming a better version of yourself, answer the following: (write in the space below)

Write down all the major events that have affected or are currently impacting you the most in your life.
(Start with most recent and work backwards)

Do you notice any recurring patterns?

What are some of the lessons you learned from what you have experienced?

You must acknowledge everything that has happened to you, accept that it happened, and then learn from it.

If you do not accept and acknowledge your experiences, you will repeat the pattern.

Do not miss your learning opportunities, choose to learn. Mistakes will always happen but learn from every situation or experience.

Next, acknowledge all the different versions of yourself.
Who was the younger version of yourself and what was your nickname?

What was your dream at that time?

Who was your next version of yourself and what was your nickname?

What makes you different from your previous version of yourself?

Now, who are you outside of your education, your title, your career? Do you know who you are? If you do not know who you are outside of a job, a relationship, or a title, then you don't know what your core needs are.

What is something you would tell your younger self?

The result of your life today is based on the information you have given your brain previously. Your behaviors are created from your thoughts and your past experiences.

So, what area has been difficult for you?

You cannot become the best version of yourself if you cannot be honest with yourself.

It takes 21 days to create and break habits, and each day is a day to become a better version of yourself to get the life you want.

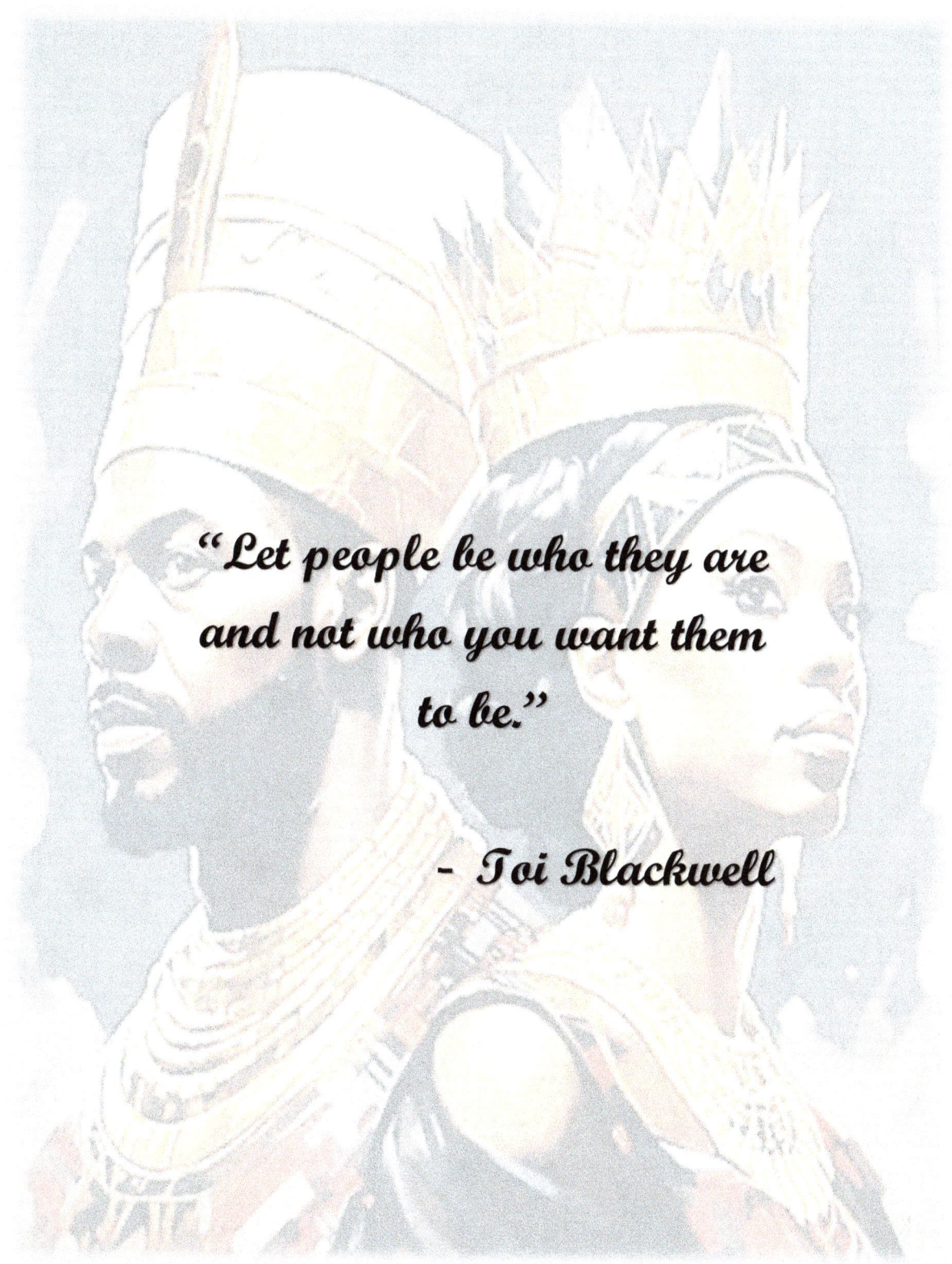

"Let people be who they are and not who you want them to be."

— Toi Blackwell

WHAT IS YOUR ATTACHMENT STYLE?

In order to become a better version of yourself you will need to determine if you have a healthy attachment style.

Based on whatever traumatic events you may have experienced in your life will result in how you interact and behave with others. Every human being is designed to receive love and give love. You are not designed to be alone. When you are alone it leads to your brain creating unhealthy coping mechanisms and the government recognizes this and uses this as a form of punishment by placing a person in isolation because human beings are designed to have interaction.

SO, WHAT IS YOUR ATTACHMENT STYLE?

There are four attachment styles in relationships.
- ❖ The first is a **secure** attachment style.
    - When you have a secure attachment style, you are able to share your feelings openly.
    - You're able to trust others and be trusted easily.
    - You give love easily and aren't afraid of intimacy.
    - You're not worried about a person leaving.

You are able to be independent, not needing validation, and won't get anxious when the person you're involved with doesn't respond immediately and feel as if they do not care about you or feel as if they will treat you like your last relationship did.

You have healed from your past traumas and no longer internalize a person's reaction to be a reflection of you. You have made the choice to stop replaying your past.

- ❖ The second is an **avoidant** attachment style.
    - o This is when your relationship is great in the beginning, you get exactly what you want, then as time goes by, you get bored and lose interest.
    - o You become distant and subconsciously build a wall to avoid a person getting too close to you.
    - o You dislike being put in a vulnerable space.
    - o You avoid taking ownership of your actions and would rather change the subject to deflect from what is really going on with you.
    - o You do not trust others.
    - o You think highly of yourself, are mostly a very high achiever, think you do not need anyone, and can take care of yourself.

This attachment style is driven by trauma that has not been addressed and healed.

It is likely that you have gotten hurt in your past, had a terrible breakup, and were cheated on. This caused the lack of trust, and negative outlook of others.

This attachment style must do the work and look inward first and determine where did the first pain come from, and not internalize it.

- ❖ The third is an **anxious** attachment style.
    - o This attachment style does not like to be alone.
    - o You find it extremely hard to be single.
    - o You often need someone to provide you with reassurance that you are loved and that the person is not going to leave you.
    - o You tend to be hard on yourself and easy on others.

This attachment style has a lot of communication conflicts in relationships because they are drawn to have more intense mood swings that demand a person's attention and feel the need to always want to fix their partner or care for them in some way. This can also be vice versa, where the person is wounded looking for a person to take care of them.

Nonetheless, it is an unhealthy attachment style that also requires reflecting and looking at yourself first to determine why and how are you reacting to other people's actions towards you.

You have to know that how a person treats you is not a reflection of you. It is a reflection of what that person has experienced and encountered in their life.

- ❖ The third is a **fearful** attachment style.
    - o Individuals with this attachment style view themselves negatively, as well as the remainder of the world in a negative way.
    - o They often think they are too broken or too wounded to be loved.
    - o They often do not like themselves or others.
    - o They do not trust others, so they hate opening up to people.

This attachment style usually thinks that all men or women are bad, and all relationships have issues and would rather remain stuck in an unhealthy relationship, because they expect for the next one to be just as bad. So at least they know the demon that they currently have then another one.

This is a clear indicator of past unhealed trauma wounds and self-reflection is needed. Learning not to place blame on yourself but acknowledge and recognize where this came from.

Becoming aware of your attachment style allows you to take the focus off others and focus on yourself.

ASSIGNMENT:

1. Look yourself in the mirror and be completely truthful with yourself.
   - Admit your failures
   - Admit your flaws
   - What you did to contribute to what you are in?

This is you acknowledging and taking accountability for your past behaviors.
Do not stay in this energy.

That version of you is not who is before you today.
That version of you is over.

2. Stand in front of a mirror, look yourself in the eyes and say:

    ➢ I love you – (7) times

    ➢ You are great – (7) times

    ➢ I love everyone and everyone loves me – (7) times

You will notice your energy and vibrations will begin to rise each time each word is spoken.

You must say these three statements out loud for your ears to hear and send back the information into your brain to believe.

Speaking in a mirror allows your eyes to see what is being said to you and send a signal back to your brain for you to know.

It now becomes your truth.

FORGIVENESS

In order for you to become a better version of yourself, you must forgive those from your past.

It could be as soon as from yesterday, last month, last year, or from your childhood, forgiveness is not for them, it is for you.

Having unforgiveness will play a role in creating unhealthy attachments with others.
When you've had to deal with being let down, or betrayed multiple times in your life, it can cause you to build walls that do not allow you to be vulnerable to people.

You build walls out of fear of only being let down again.
You stop asking for help.

If you have this behavior, you have trauma that needs to be forgiven, so you can heal and trust others.

Whatever pain that is not resolved in one relationship will always follow you into your next relationship and you will continue to repeat unhealthy patterns.

Give yourself closure without an apology.

You only have control over yourself and your actions.

No one else.

It would be nice to receive an apology, but guess what?

No one owes you anything.

You may think that you are healed from a situation or a person because you choose not to think about it.

However, if you bring it to the forefront of your mind and it still upsets you, then you are not fully healed in that area, and you must continue to do the work.

ASSIGNMENT:

Take your power back. Answer the following questions:

1. Acknowledge and write down who or what has hurt you?

2. Why did it hurt you?

3. How did it make you feel? Be truthful with yourself. Did you feel ashamed, guilty, less than, not enough, powerless?

Once you acknowledge the feeling behind the offense, that is your starting point.

You are worth more than having anxiety, stress, or being depressed because of someone else's behaviors, and how they chose to treat you.

It could have been your mother, your father, your siblings, or a past relationship.

You do not carry someone else's choice.

How a person treats you is not a reflection of you, it is a reflection of themselves.

Now that you are on your journey to becoming a better version of yourself, you are creating habits to reprogram your mind and stop accepting toxic behaviors in your life.

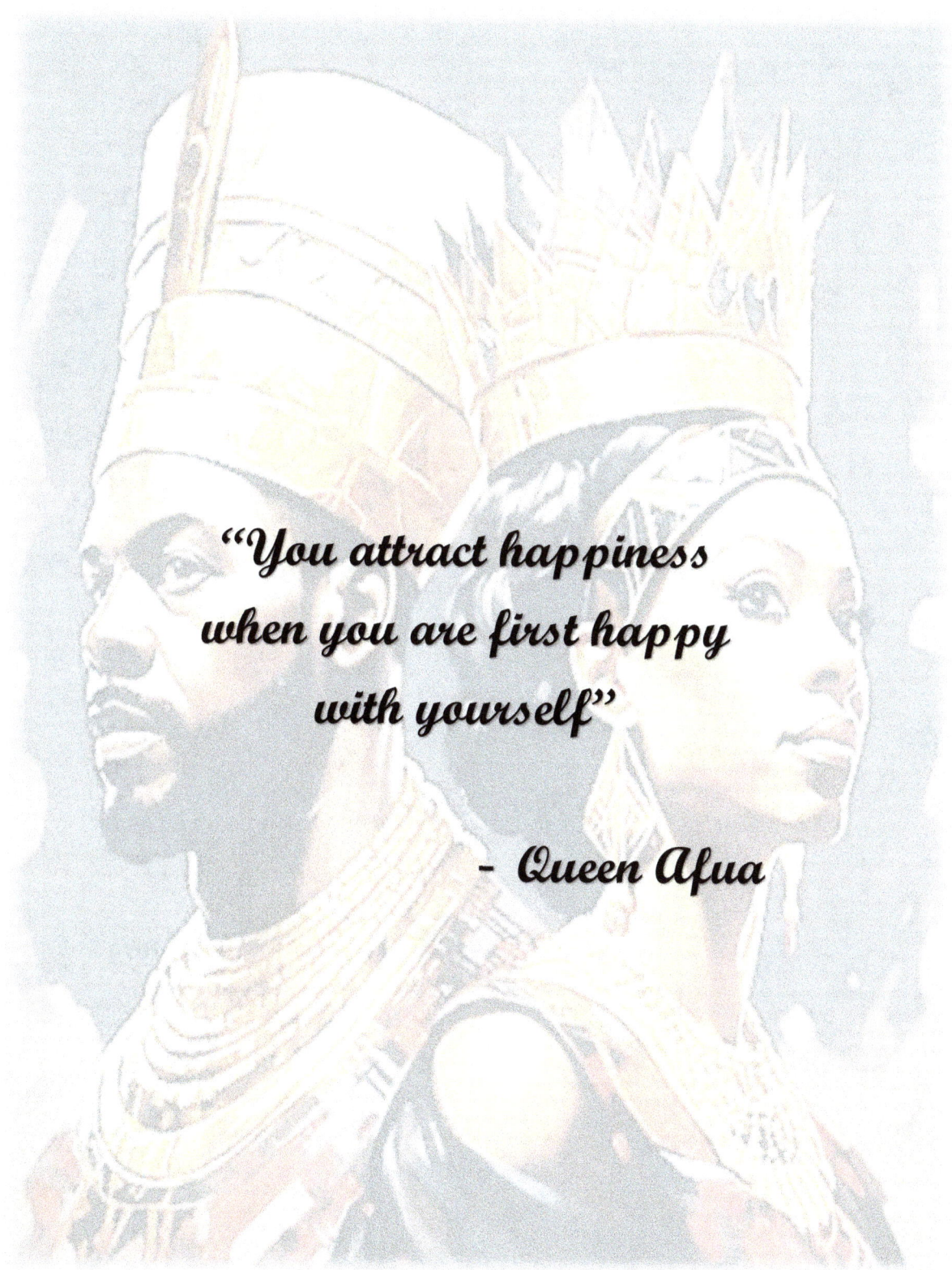

"You attract happiness when you are first happy with yourself"

– Queen Afua

REPROGRAM YOUR RESPONSE

Never look at what you have had to experience as if it was meant to destroy you.

It is not.

Every experience we have had to encounter is meant to develop us to learn from and grow from.

When things happen, it's your reaction that causes a change in your reality.

It has nothing to do with what actually happened.

For example, if you get a flat tire, the old version of you might've gotten stressed and upset. However, when you get stressed out your body sends out energy signals of fear and that is how you attract more negative energy into your life. It creates a chain reaction, because it all starts in your mind first, thinking of all the possibilities of what can go wrong and what is going wrong. Setting your mind to consciously think of what happened in the past and subconsciously think of the worst.

So, it is important to learn to reprogram your reactions to respond in a way through love of yourself and to others. It has to be automatic from you doing the work by acknowledging your behaviors and consciously changing your response when difficult situations arise. Your subconscious mind knows that everything you experience is not working against you. It is working for you.

ASSIGNMENT:

Develop an **automatic response** to all situations by training yourself to say,

"Everything is going according to plan and is working out perfectly with ease."

Positive information has to be embedded into your brain so your brain can have positive information to respond in a situation.

So instead of thinking negatively, you could choose to change your perspective that the flat tire could have been to prevent you from experiencing something worse and could have been the very thing that saved your life.

We are our toughest critics.

Be kind to yourself and give yourself grace.

Your thoughts create your reality.

Change out the old information for new information and give your brain better choices to choose from to become a better version of yourself.

CREATE NEW HABITS

Habits are repeated behaviors that begin from trial and error.

As you become a newer version of yourself you must develop new habits.

ASSIGNMENT: Take an assessment of your life.

- What would you like to do more of?

- What do you see yourself having?

- What type of friends would you like to have?
  Do an audit of your friends. You are the average of the 5 people you spend the most time with.

- What are you doing for your self-care? (ie. meditation)

- What are you doing for your self-maintenance? (ie. massages)

- What would you like to be doing for money?

Embrace change.
Embrace who you want to become.

Embrace your transition to becoming a better version of yourself.

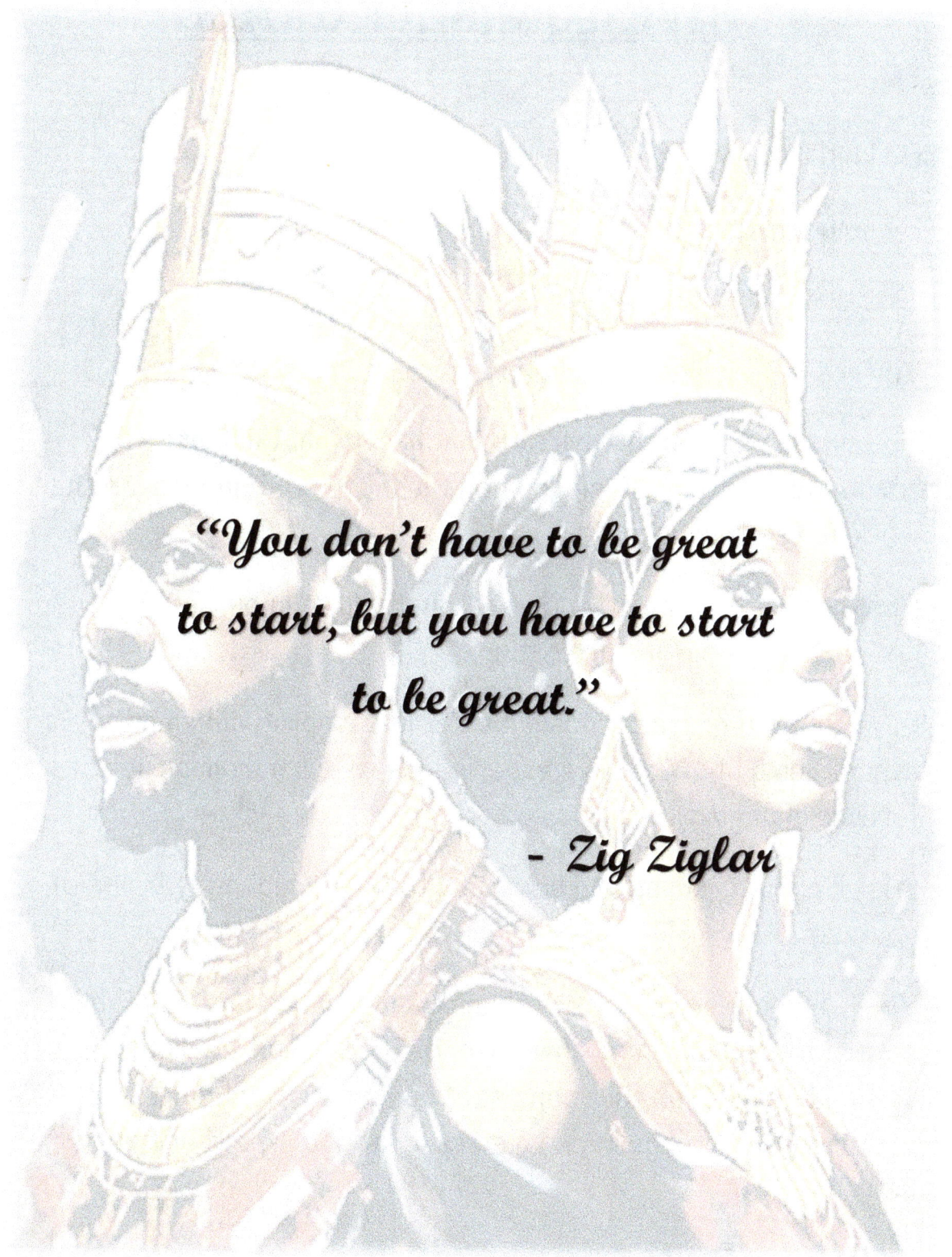

"You don't have to be great to start, but you have to start to be great."

- Zig Ziglar

GIVE YOURSELF GRACE

Be kind to yourself.

Be kind to others.

Give you and others grace.

You are not God and should not judge.

You may want to resort back to whom and what you are comfortable with because you don't want to continuously do the work and self-reflect.

Self-reflect and pay attention to what you tell yourself, how you are behaving, how you are acting.

Give yourself grace because you are just a spiritual being that is experiencing life. You have experiences to learn from as you are forever changing and growing.

It is all about growing and becoming to be the highest version of yourself.

You can continue your life path with a Human connection that consist of having worry, anxiety, and stress about everything, or in a spiritual connection that consist of going with the flow, listening to your inner spirit knowing no matter what you experience you will be ok.

This month, reframe your perspective in all situations.
Try to see all sides before assuming.

Change out the old information in your brain for new information and give your brain better choices to choose from to create the reality that you want.

It's all about growing and becoming a better version of yourself one day at a time.

GET INTO ALIGNMENT

There is always a reason for where you are today.
Your thinking. Your habits. Your distractions.

Listen to your intuition. Believe your intuition. Your intuition is your inner voice, which is also your spirit, that will speak to you and let you know what you should be doing and what you should not be doing. You will either feel comfortable in situations or you will not.

We are here to love and give love.

We each have an assignment and are here to figure out what we are supposed to be doing. Your assignment may not be grand, but there is a reason for your talent and a reason for your skills.

Do not live in fear, based on your past experiences.
Do not overthink what you feel intuitively.
Your intuition will speak to you. It's on you to follow it.

When you do not listen to your intuition, you could be missing out on the very thing that God has been trying to bring into your life or save you from.

You aren't designed to remain the same. You are meant to grow and learn on your journey. Some people aren't meant to remain in your life, and you should not feel bad about it.

Some of us make permanent decisions based on situations we were only meant to learn a lesson from, and if we would've listened to our intuition, our results would be different.

ASSIGNMENT:

How to get into alignment?

1. Begin scheduling time in your day to be still. If you are always doing, you first need to learn how to not "do". Allow yourself to be silent and connect with yourself to reflect on your emotions, the things you've been through, and what your desires are.

2. Take inventory of your friends and choose friends that are on the same journey as you.

3. When problems arise, instead of getting upset, try and see what the lesson is.

Your life is always speaking to you. You must be still so you can get into alignment.

"Do not take anything personal,
Do not make any assumptions,
Be aware of the words you speak,
Make an effort to do your best."

— The Four Agreements
By Don Miguel Ruiz

THE POWER OF DETACHMENT

When you stop caring about the outcome you become a better version of yourself.

When you put excessive energy into something you give off a desperation frequency, but when you don't give off that frequency, you are not tied to the results.

This version of yourself can remain in the present flow state. No matter the outcome of a situation, you will be ok.

Detach from the job

Detach from the relationship

Detach from things not working out exactly how you envisioned.

When you put the best version of yourself first, you try and give it your all, you can rest knowing you have done all that you could do.

ASSIGNMENT:

Detach from how something ends.

God knows what you desire the most, and you have to be ok with knowing your outcome is designed to make you a better version of yourself.

Your experiences are not designed to hurt you, they are truly designed to make you better.

Learn from your experiences and work on yourself.

You only have control over yourself.

RELEASE CONTROL

God is in control.

God has the final say.

God has divine timing and divine order for when things are going to happen in your life.

You have to be patient for what you are waiting for.

Take an assessment of yourself and determine why is it hard for you to let go?

When something is cooking, you have to wait.
Life is the same way.
You cannot eat something when it is not ready.

Thinking too much about your future will bring anxiety and stress into your life.

Be patient.

Patience produces peace, and peace will guard your heart and mind.

ASSIGNMENT:

Based on what you are experiencing, answer the following:
(write in the space below)

What are you learning?

What area are you healing?

Declare you have peace over your heart, peace over your mind and the ability to release control.

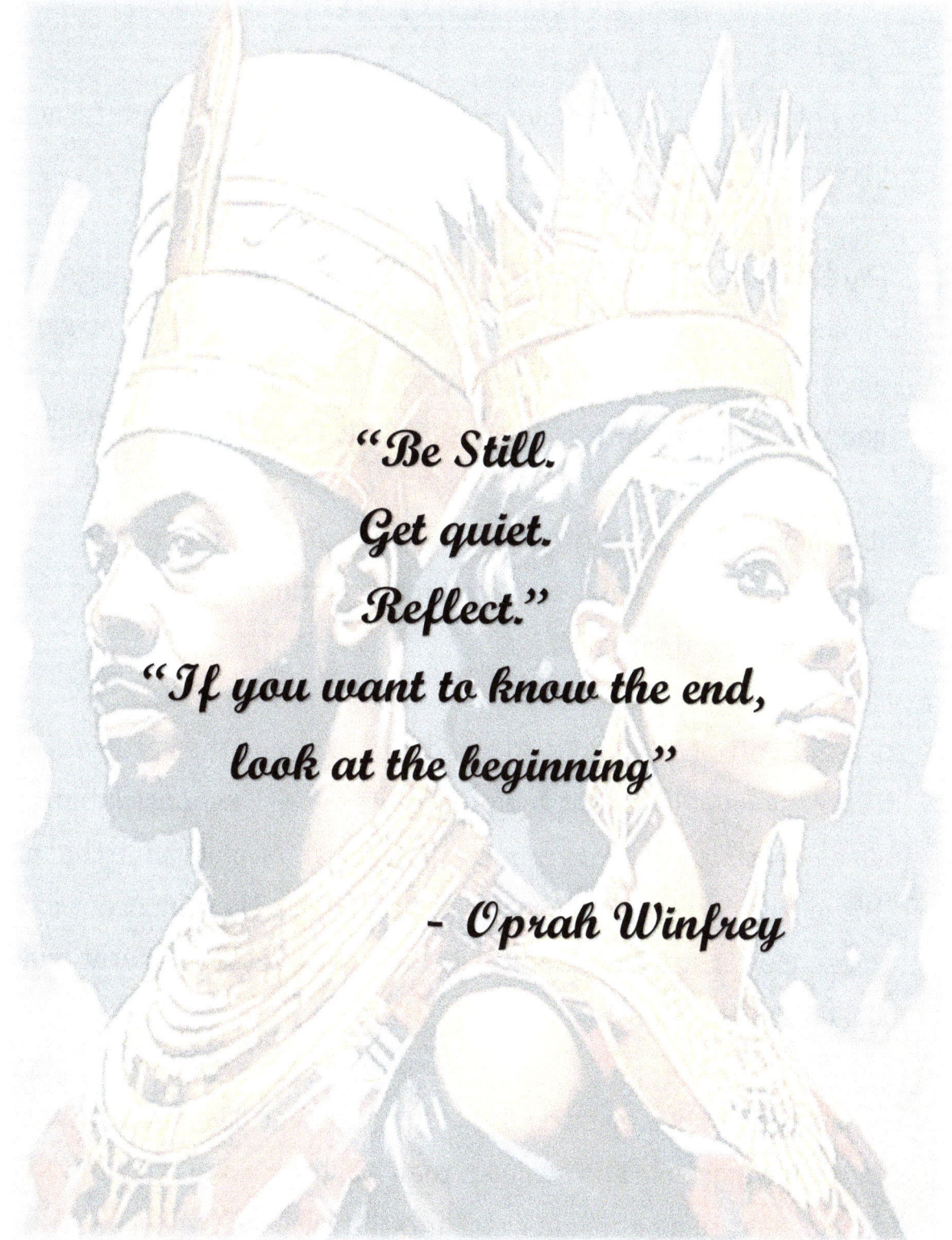

"Be Still.
Get quiet.
Reflect."
"If you want to know the end,
look at the beginning"

— Oprah Winfrey

YOUR LEGACY

Do not allow what you have experienced in your life to determine your children's future.

Parents have a tendency to project their feelings and make choices for their children based off their own past traumas and what they experienced growing up. For example, not allowing your child to play a sport because you had an injury from a sport.

It is important for children to know they are loved, for them to develop self-value and self-worth by trusting the decisions the parents allow them to make.

Parents often become so focused on the things they provide as expressions of love that they forget it is their responsibility to also communicate love verbally. It's crucial for children to hear the words "I love you" regularly, as this helps them incorporate those words into their core belief system and stop generational unhealthy habits.

Some parents become too busy trying to over give what they didn't have growing up or make their children's lives too easy losing sight of what made them into the parents they are today.

ASSIGNMENT:

Take time to self-reflect on your parenting.
(write in the spaces below)

1. What emotional legacy are you leaving your children?

2. How do you know that your children feel loved, feel safe, and feel protected?

3. Do they feel that they are competent to make choices for themselves so they can develop self-value and not become codependent?

YOUR PURPOSE

Everyone has a bigger purpose in their life.
You have to first want it and be open to receiving it.

Look at what you are doing.

Do you love what you are doing?

Does it bring you joy?

How does it help others?

When you are purpose-driven, you do not need anyone's approval.
You only need support.

Do not expect everyone to understand your vision. Some will support you, some will not, but do not leave your vision, even if you must stand by yourself.

(write in the space below)
What do you think your purpose is?

What are you doing to become better in this area?

You aren't designed to remain the same. You are meant to grow and learn to discover what is your life's purpose. Everyone has a skill set and a talent.

Your purpose will not feel or seem like work. You will be fulfilled, and your needs will be met.

You will not change who you are for others but for your self-development. You will remain true to yourself. True to your core belief system.

You have a purpose for your life.

You are here for a reason.

THANK YOU GOD

- Today I thank you God for a great day.
- Today I ask for forgiveness for my past and for any negative energy to be released from my heart.
- Today I thank you for a healthy body.
- Today I thank you for unexpected miracles happening to me.
- Today I thank you that I am safe.
- Today I thank you for the ability to make money and enjoy what I do.
- Today I thank you for my happiness and my life is full of joy.
- Today I thank you for my life aligning into the way you want it to be.
- Today I thank you that my heart and spirit is full of love, it is healed, and it is at peace.
- Today I thank you for protecting me from any negativity.
- Today I thank you for the knowledge of knowing that what a person does, has nothing to do with me and I do not take things personally.

- ❖ Today I thank you for the strength to forgive those who have wronged me, and I choose to love them anyway.
- ❖ Today I thank you for fighting my battles.
- ❖ Today I thank you for allowing me to be a blessing to someone with my gifts.
- ❖ Today I thank you for loving relationships.
- ❖ Today I thank you that my mind and spirit are at peace.
- ❖ Today I thank you for not feeling lonely, and I feel loved.
- ❖ Today I thank you for all things that are working for my good.
- ❖ Today I thank you that everything is working out better than I dreamed of.
- ❖ Today I thank you that I am surrounded by the right people.
- ❖ Today I simply thank you for your grace over my life.

Believe these things and more, even if they haven't happened yet.

Be specific with what you are believing in God for.

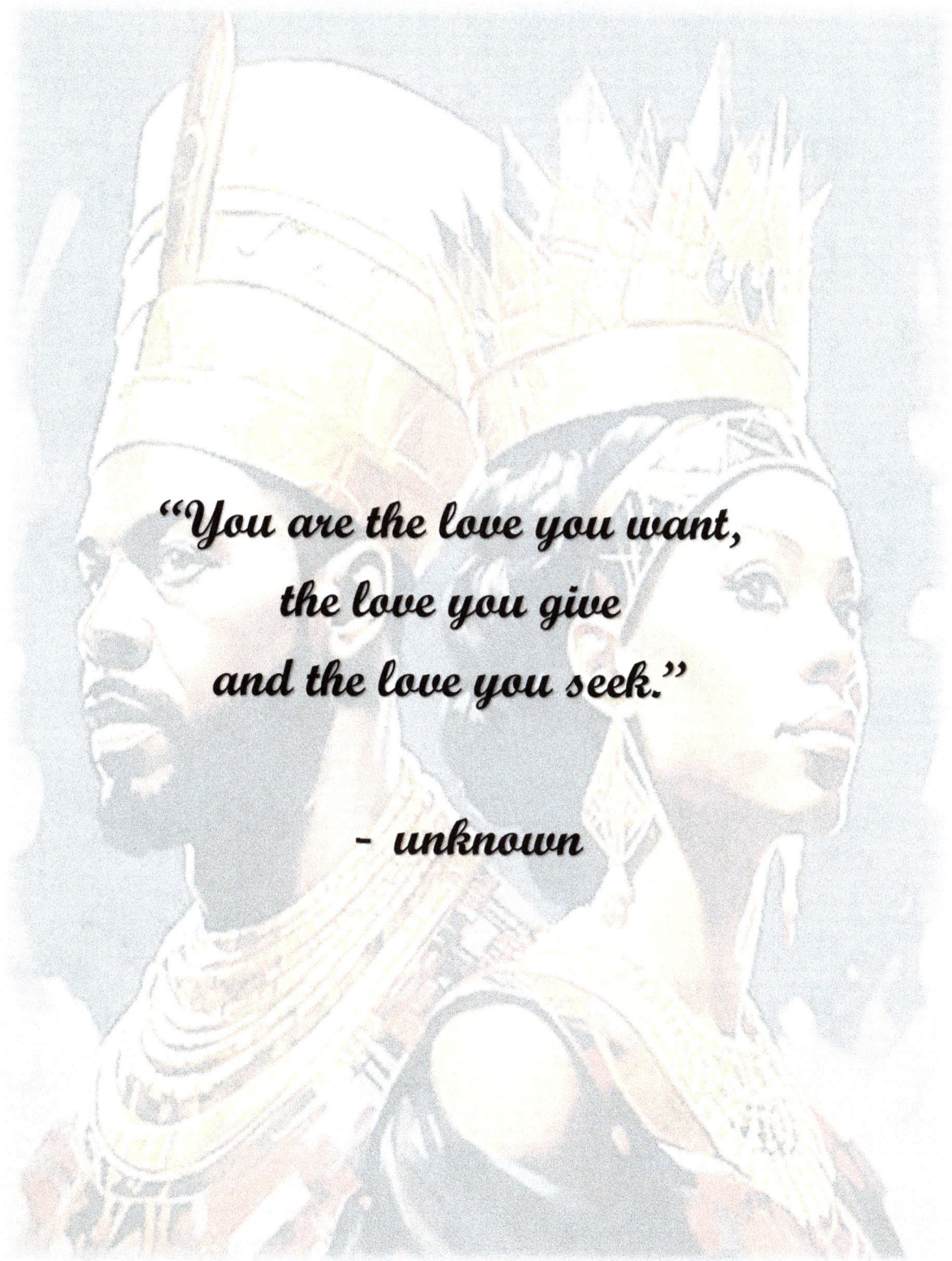

"You are the love you want,
the love you give
and the love you seek."

- unknown

YOUR NEW YEAR

As you continue on your healing journey, God will constantly give you new visions for you to carry out.

It is important to sit still, listen, and begin to move.

God will provide you with the information and the tools needed to carry the vision into existence.

It is on you to know that you are capable of carrying it out.

You have to believe in yourself, first.
Change always starts from within.

If you do not carry out the vision, the vision will be given to someone else. That is why you will see many with the same ideas. However, the delivery will not be the same.

Everyone is unique. So do not get discouraged if you have the same idea as someone else. The vision that God has shown you is uniquely created for you to carry out, it will not be like others if you remain true to yourself and be authentic.

LOVE ADVICE

So often, so many people when they love a person, they think it is about them. Who they are, how they make us feel, and what they do, but in reality, when you love someone, it is about yourself.

It shows how you are capable of loving another person, it shows your vulnerable areas, your character, and where you have experienced lack.

When you enter into a relationship with someone, you are really in a relationship with yourself through a physical connection with another person.

That person will either pull out your very best or they will pull out your worst, however, it is your choice on what you allow to be pulled out of you.
You control your behavior.
You control how you allow another person to treat you.
The love that you are able to give someone, comes from within yourself first.

How you allow others to treat you, will be a visual representation of how you love yourself. You will know when it feels right.
Your natural capacity to be open, available, and vulnerable, will feel like your own love from within.

Do not focus externally.

God made you whole.

Whatever you feel you need from another person, you have to know that you have it all within yourself.

Do not attach any lack you carry from your past to another person. It is not theirs to carry with you.

You must do your own inner work.

<u>First</u>, start by figuring out your triggers and asking yourself, why do you have those triggers?

<u>Second</u>, acknowledge and confront your pain. Acknowledge your feelings. Both men and women are both spiritual beings in human flesh. You have feelings and are entitled to acknowledge when you have been mistreated, felt unseen, unsafe, or unheard.

<u>Third</u>, make the choice to move forward and not focus on your past. Anytime a negative or sad thought comes into your mind, you make the choice to not focus on it. You make the choice to change what you focus on.

Give yourself the permission to stop reflecting on your past and know the love that someone gives you, is really, you loving yourself.

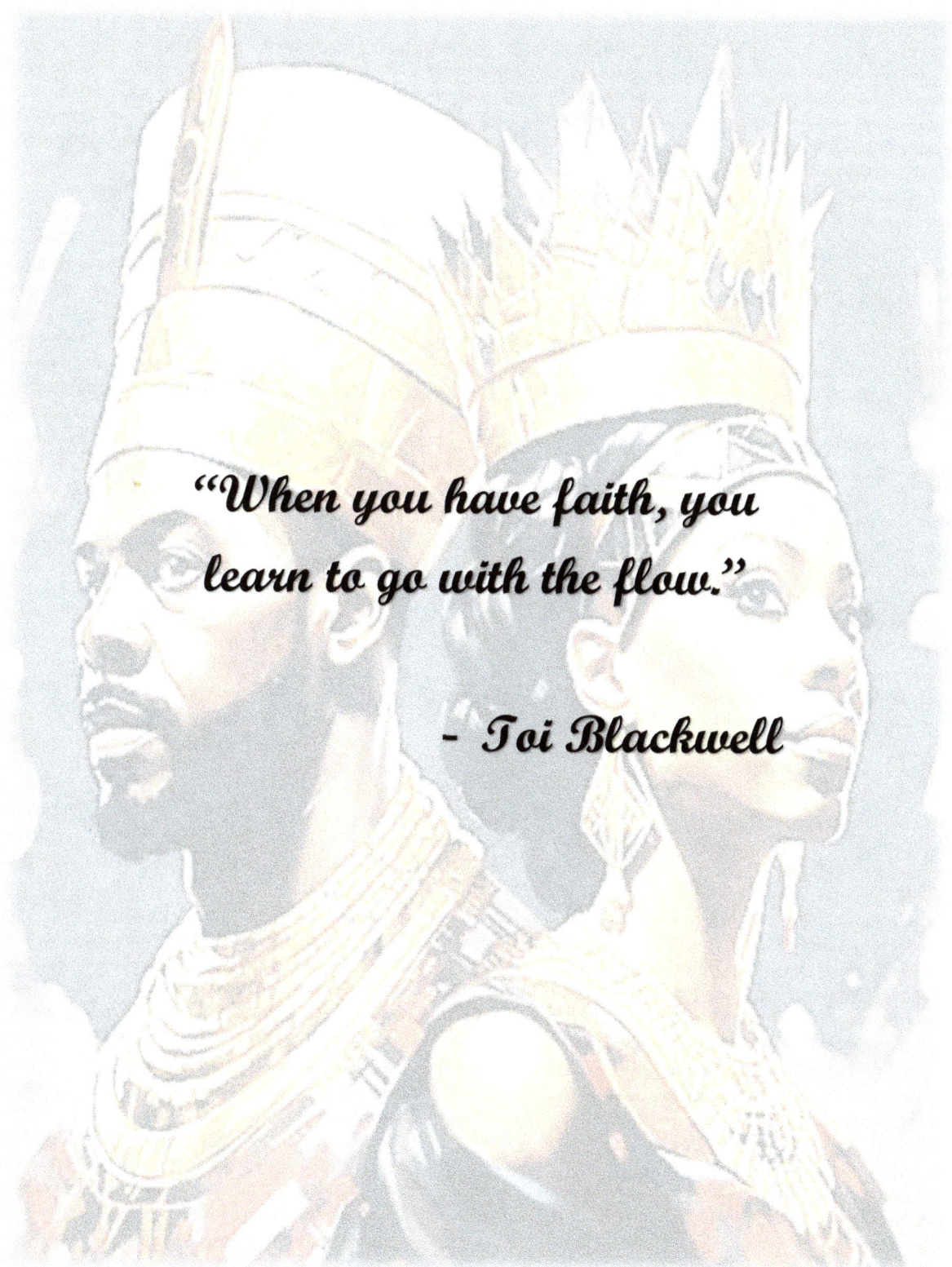

"When you have faith, you learn to go with the flow."

— Toi Blackwell

YOUR INNER CHILD

The inner child in you knows who you are and who you want to become. The secret to your life's journey is within the inner child inside of you.

Ask the child in you, who did you want to be.
Your inner child knows the answer. Your inner child knows who you are destined to become.

Over the years you ignore your inner child's desires and develop wounds on your inner child through painful experiences. It is not until you are made to feel safe that you are able to go deep within and remember your inner child's desires and bring him or her back to the forefront within you.

Develop a relationship with your inner child and they will show you the way. They will show you what it is you are supposed to be doing.

Everything lies within you.
You have to be fearless.
You have to be bold.

Look within and ask the inner child in you to show you your vision.

YOUR GREAT ENDEAVOR

What is your great endeavor of your life?

Your destiny, your life path, is meant to be uncomfortable.
It's not always meant to be easy.
If things were always easy you would never grow.

You are meant to have challenges in order to step into your greatest path.

If something is meant for you, God will give you a clear vision for it.
If you are unclear, uncertain, then it might mean it is not for you or not the right time for it.

When you are moving in the right direction, God will give you clarity and specific instructions for it.
When you are on the right path, you won't have to wonder if you are on the right path.

You will be satisfied.
You will be fulfilled.
You may feel a little uncomfortable at first because it is a new feeling, but it will bring you happiness.

YOUR PATH

No one is completely healed.

People must enter your life and encounter situations with you to determine how far you have evolved on your path.

You are constantly growing, changing, and experiencing life daily.

Your path is about discovering yourself in new ways.

As you are moving forward on your path, you will experience (3) phases, and each phase creates a new version of yourself:

1st Phase:	Clear out old attachments.
	Clear out things or people, that are keeping you confused, fearful, unhappy, or unfocused.
	This is the uncomfortable and painful phase, because you have to clear out what has been comfortable for you.
	You must release what does not serve you on the path for where you are trying to go.

2nd Phase:	Once you have released negative ways of thinking, negative energies, and negative attachments, you are now clear to attract positive energy in. Your body will attract prosperity, luck, love, and good fortune. This is the magnetic stage in your life. Although it is not about money, luck, or love, they are a byproduct of the positive energy.
3rd Phase:	You are in alignment. Your frequency naturally attracts everything your soul needs because you have made the choice to do what God has intended for your life. The work that you are now doing, others are benefiting from it. You are causing chain reactions in others, and now, because of your work, they are impacting others. One person's positive change will change the environment around them, which causes positive change around another person's environment, and eventually the world. Change is a choice that starts with self.

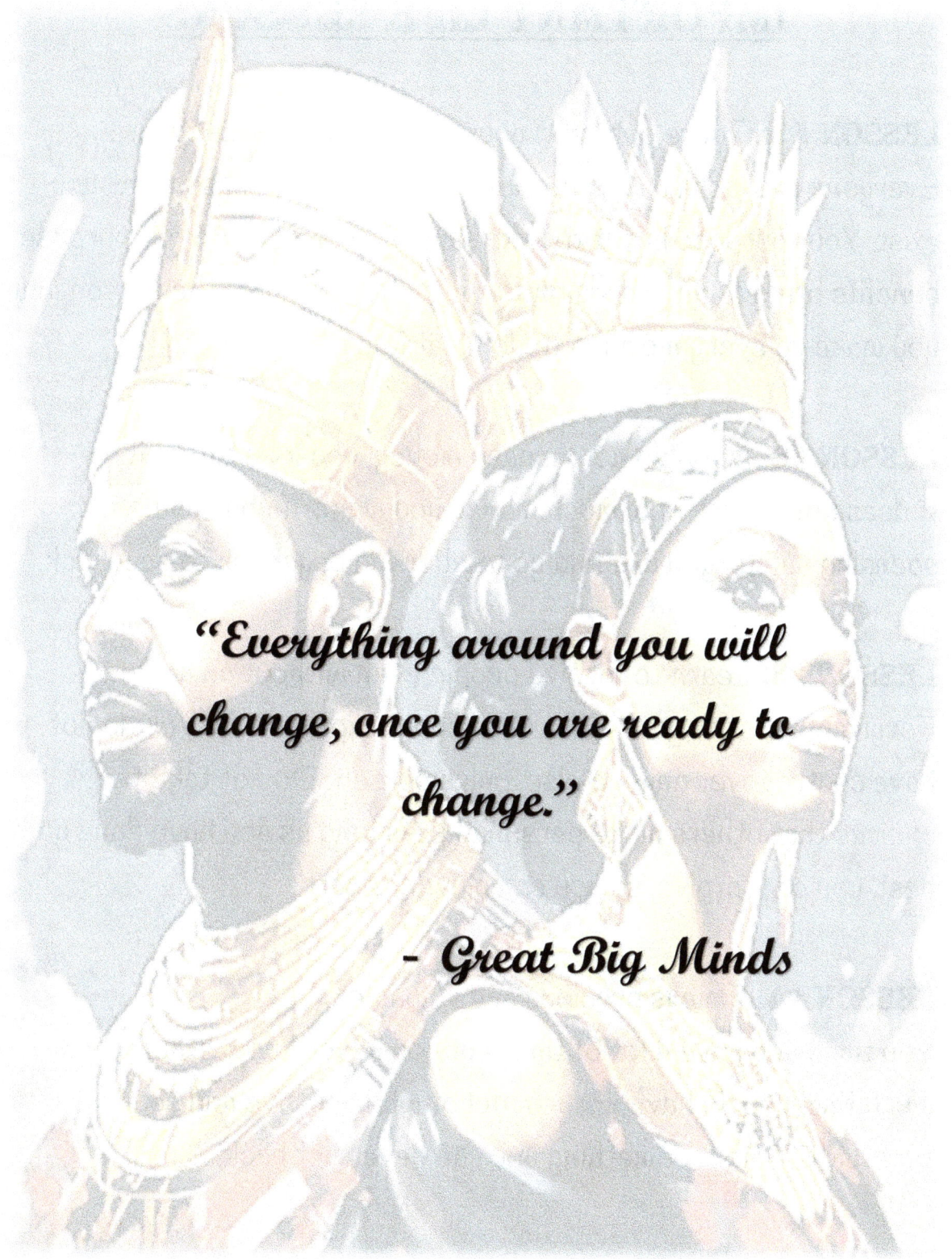

"Everything around you will change, once you are ready to change."

- Great Big Minds

IMPORTANT LIFE LESSONS

LESSON #1: Figure out what your gifts and your talents are. Everyone was born with a purpose and there is a reason why you exist. Your purpose is not to take care of your family. Your purpose benefits others. Have a vision for your life and know the reason why you wake up every morning to do what it is you are doing.

LESSON #2: If you do not manage money, you won't have it. It does not matter how much money you make, if you have poor spending habits, you will find yourself living paycheck to paycheck.

LESSON #3: Learn to forgive people even without an apology. Forgiveness is for yourself. Life is about experiences. You do not have control over anyone else, only yourself. Do not take the choices that others make personally. As long as you have done your best, you can forgive, so you can move forward.

LESSON #4: Time is precious and valuable.
You think you have a lot of time, but you never know exactly how much time you do have. Be mindful of who you give and spend your time with. Time is something you can never get back.

LESSON #5: You are not alone in your challenges.
Everyone experiences challenges in something. No one is perfect. Everyone will experience obstacles in life they must get through, as every obstacle shapes and mold you into who you are today.

LESSON #6: Have compassion and empathy for others.
Dealing with people can be hard. At work you will learn, it's not the job, it's managing and working with people. It's important to learn to be understanding of what others may be experiencing or have experienced in their past.

LESSON#7: Everyone is given opportunities.
You cannot blame other people for where you are in life today. You must take accountability for your actions. Take responsibility for the choices you have made. The energy you spend finding reasons for your decisions, is energy you could use to put back in to yourself.

LESSON #8: Focus on yourself
Do not worry about what others are doing, and why they have the things that they have. You do not know a person's full life story. You do not know the struggles they had to endure or the tears they have cried behind closed doors. Learn to always be kind to others.

LESSON #9: Love yourself

You cannot love others, if you do not first love yourself. Despite any negative or unpleasant experiences from your past, you must understand that how someone else treated you is a reflection of them. When you love yourself, you create and maintain healthy boundaries with yourself and how you allow others to treat you. The cycle of life is about learning to love and to give love to others. When you love yourself so much, you can't help but to see love in others.

LESSON #10: It's never too late to grow

Your growth will build your character. How you start in life does not have to determine where you end. If you do not have the information that you seek around you, you must seek it for yourself. Everything starts with you. When you are ready to change, then everything around you will change.

"Do not live your life in fear.

Fear of getting hurt
Fear of failing
or
Fear of losing.

Life is worth living in your truth,
being your authentic self"

– Toi Blackwell

IMPERFECTLY PERFECT

When you continuously face the same situation and experience the same type of energy but in different bodies, this means you are missing lessons.

You are repeating cycles out of habit, because you have not learned the lesson yet.

You are in fear of something, and until you face your fear, you will continue to repeat situations.

Whatever you are in fear of, you must know it starts from the very beginning of who first introduced you to what love is for you.
Your mother and your father. Present or absent.

Love is then shaped and molded after that.
What you experienced from the start became your initial core belief and foundation of love, that led you to where you are today.

So, you must first speak to that little boy inside of you, or little girl inside of you, and tell him or her, what you would've liked to have been told at that time.

Tell them now, that they are safe, that they are loved, that they are smart, that they are enough.

What you are facing today comes from your core belief system, and you must know that you do not have to live your life in fear from your past.

Your value, your worth, is not tied to anything you have experienced in your past.

It doesn't matter how long it takes to heal the little person in you, just that you are now able to put a smile on his or her face.

Everything is not what it seems. You are doing a great job!

Just as babies that are born into this world are instantly valuable, being a baby, not having to do anything.

You are valuable.

You are imperfectly perfect just as you are!

NOTES

Sit with yourself and write your thoughts.
Write down the first thing that comes to your mind.

NOTES

Continue to write whatever comes to mind.